KITTERY TO THE KENNEBUNKS

A PHOTOGRAPHIC PORTRAIT

First published in the United States of America by
PilotPress Publishers, Inc.
110 Westchester Road
Newton, Massachusetts 02458
Telephone: (617) 332-0703
www.PilotPress.com
and
Twin Light Publishers, Inc.
Ten Hale Street
Rockport, Massachusetts 01966
Telephone: (978) 546-7398

ISBN 1-885435-08-8

10 9 8 7 6 5 4 3 2 1

Designer: Leeann Leftwich
            Email: clldesign@aol.com

Cover image: Bernie O'Doherty

Back cover image: Edgar Ohman

Front flap images: (top) Robert Dennis
                (bottom) Leanne Cusimano

Back flap images: (top) Carol Hartley Bellows
                (bottom) Neil Falby

KITTERY TO THE KENNEBUNKS

A PHOTOGRAPHIC PORTRAIT

PILOTPRESS PUBLISHERS • TWIN LIGHTS PUBLISHERS

MAINE

95 Exit 3

35

Maine Turnpike

Arundel Barn Playhouse

Kennebunk

Brick Store Museum

Exit 2 **1**

Seashore Trolley Museum

Wells Research Reserve at Laudholm Farm

9

Kennebunkport

9

Wells

Wells Beach

Rachel Carson Wildlife Refuge

Maritime Productions

Goose Rocks Beach

Moody Beach

Mother's Beach

Goat Island Lighthouse

Walker's Point

95

Footbridge Beach

Gooch's Beach

Arundel Beach

Ogunquit

Ogunquit Beach

Perkins Cove

Ogunquit Playhouse

1

Exit 1 Exit 2 Exit 3 Exit 4

1A

Short Sands Beach

Toll Booth

York

Nubble Light

Old York Historic Sites

Long Sands Beach

Kittery

York Harbor Beach

103

Boon Island Lighthouse

Fort McClary

Crescent Beach

Portsmouth NH

Whale Back Lighthouse

Fort Foster

Map courtesy of the
Southern Maine Coast Tourism Association
(800) 639-2442 or
www.southernmainecoast.com

TABLE *of* CONTENTS

FOREWORD

PilotPress Publishers and Twin Lights Publishers are pleased to bring to you this pictorial portrait of the southern Maine coast.

We started development of this book with the concept that there are many amateur, semi-professional, and professional photographers who have taken some wonderful pictures and would be interested in having their work published. The book presents many outstanding photographs of the Kittery to Kennebunk area.

These photographs are representative of the area. We ask that you view them with the same enthusiasm and excitement experienced by the photographers who live in or who visited the area and were prompted to record their memories on film. In many cases, the photographers have shared their personal thoughts about the selected pictures and we have included many of these thoughts as part of our captions. We hope this adds to your appreciation of the images, prompts you to visit the area and enhances your own experience and memories.

We would like to congratulate all whose work was selected for this book and, in particular, we would like to highlight the following photographers.

Bernie O'Doherty, *Cape Porpoise Dawn,* cover and page 7. Mr. O'Doherty began his career in filmmaking working on the 007 movie "On Her Majesty's Secret Service." His work is also represented with Jacques Cousteau, 60 Minutes, Harlan County USA, National Geographic, ABC Sports, and many commercials. He has studied at Emerson College with award-winning photographer David Akiba. Mr. O'Doherty is a member of the Society of Motion Picture and Television Engineers and was co-founder of The Atlanta Film Institute, where photography and filmmaking were taught and he is a 1998 Academy Award nominee. He is currently Film Technical Supervisor at Emerson College, Boston MA.

CONTEST WINNER
Bernie O'Doherty
Cape Porpoise Dawn

Edgar Ohman, *Christmas on the Nubble* lives in Cape Neddick, Maine and has had a long-time interest in color slide photography. Mr. Ohman is a member of the Yankee Chapter of the Photographic Society of America and a member of a local camera club in his hometown of Brockton, Massachusetts.

Neil Falby, *Foggy Wash Day*, is a thirty-year resident of Natick, Massachusetts who has been traveling to the southern Maine coast on a frequent basis over the same time period. Neil's photo collection now includes subjects from virtually every harbor and inlet from Kittery to Kennebunk, and he knows the area like the back of his hand.

A self-taught photographer, he has honed his skills by studying photographic journals, sharing experiences with other photographers and most important of all, learning from continual practice...practice...and more practice!

TOP
SECOND PLACE WINNER
Edgar Ohman
Christmas on the Nubble

THIRD PLACE WINNER
Neil Falby
Foggy Wash Day

ACKNOWLEDGMENTS

The publishers would like to acknowledge many people who helped with this book.

In particular, we would thank Doug Porter, Director of the Gateway to Maine Chamber of Commerce, for many photographs and encouragement. Visit the web site at www.gatewaytomaine.org.

To Larry, Marcia and Tracy Smith of Ogunquit Camera in Ogunquit and Ocean Exposure in Kennebunkport for their much-appreciated time and effort in helping judge our photos.

To the Southern Maine Coast Tourism Association for the use of its regional map. Contact it at (800) 639-2442 or visit its web site at www.southernmainecoast.com.

To Maine Sunshine, Inc. for its assistance in the development of the area descriptions. Pick up the Maine Sunshine Guide for valuable information on the area. Contact it at (207) 594-8074, Sunshine@midcoast.com or visit the web site at www.mainesunshine.com

And finally, to Brenda Swithenbank for continued suggestions, support and encouragement.

GREATER KITTERY

Kittery, at the southeastern tip of Maine, greets visitors to the Pine Tree State with hearty downeast hospitality. Maine's oldest town, Kittery was first settled in 1623. It is a town with many personalities; it has a long and proud history of shipbuilding and support for the naval fleet. While it is home to some 120 name brand factory outlet stores lining Maine Route 1, its shady streets and stately seafarer homes evoke a bygone time.

Kittery is home to two forts and several museums. The town is graced with many fine homes and buildings of historic and stately architecture from the 17th, 18th and 19th centuries. Stop by the 1760 Lady Pepperrell House and the 1730 First Congregational Church on scenic Route 103. Fort McClary is a state memorial on a 27-acre site, and Fort Foster, on a nearby 90-acre island, is now a park operated by the Town of Kittery.

Enjoy a drive or stroll along Kittery's many tidal river areas to Kittery Point where you will find brightly colored boats rocking gently in their sheltered moorings. Sample the range of local Atlantic seafood delights, including a first taste of sweet Maine lobster, at one of the many harborside restaurants.

West of Route 1 is the quiet countryside of Eliot, an old New England town with a rural landscape and colorful farm stands just a few miles inland. Located to the west of Kittery along the Piscataqua River's northern shore, Eliot was once a part of Kittery but incorporated as an independent town in 1810.

Eliot has its own unique style and tempo and many fine examples of New England architecture among its homes and public buildings. Attractions in the Eliot area include the Fogg Library, listed on the National Register of Historic Places, the William Fogg House, the Dr. Willis Homestead, the 1768 Libby Home, a former roadside tavern, and the site of the first Quaker meeting House (1776).

Mary Ellen McCollumn
Dinghies at the Kittery Town Dock
Kittery Point
Walk out on the dock past these small boats to see the pleasure boats moored in the cove and watch the lobstermen unloading their catch. While in this area visit Frisbee's General Store, the oldest family-run store in the country.

TOP
Mary Ellen McCollumn
Fort McClary, Kittery Point
On Route 103, as seen across the Piscataqua River from Kittery Town Dock. Fort McClary, dating back to 1690 was originally known as Pepperell's Garrison and is believed to have existed to protect the settlers from "unexpected" Indian attacks. It was used in five wars to protect the entrance to the river. Fort McClary is now a State Park.

Doug Porter
Kittery Outlet Shopping
Over one hundred and twenty outlet stores attract shoppers of every age to the Maine seacoast every day.

RIGHT
Edgar Ohman
Chauncey Creek, Kittery Point
Stony tree-lined inlet separating Kittery Point from Gerrish Island. Several small lobstering piers dot the shoreline. Photo taken from the well-known Chauncey Creek Lobster Pier where you can enjoy the view and eat "lobster in the rough."

Julie Loneske
Salt Marsh Game Reserve on
Route 103 at the York / Kittery Line
*The solitude and beauty of the cold
gray mid-November day in Maine.*

LEFT
Julie Loneske
Salt Marsh Game Reserve
*Abandoned fisherman's hut perhaps
used before this salt marsh became
a fragile and endangered area.*

RIGHT
Mary Ellen McCollumn
Old Graveyard Along Piscataqua
River at Kittery Point
*The Congregational Church grave-
yard on Route 103 in Kittery Point
across from the oldest church in
Maine, built in 1730. A walk
through the graveyard affords a
spectacular water view at any time
of year. Old gravestones date to the
1700's and show the names of
many famous and early residents of
Kittery including the Church's first
Pastor and Deacon. The old graveyard is, according to local lore, said
to be haunted.*

RIGHT, BELOW
Julie Loneske
Salt Marsh Game Reserve on
Route 103 at the York / Kittery Line

Doug Porter
Chauncey Creek

Chauncey Creek in Kittery Point remains untouched by over development. The Route 103 area of Kittery Point is great for bicycling with the family. The road leads to secluded beaches and historic forts, and you will enjoy miles of natural Maine beauty.

LEFT
Doug Porter
Whaleback Light at the entrance to Portsmouth Harbor brings you to Kittery, the gateway to Maine.

Doug Porter

The scenic views of Fort Foster await your exploration and enjoyment.

RIGHT
Doug Porter

The fishing pier at Fort Foster in Kittery Point jets out into the Atlantic Ocean. Sit and enjoy fishing boats as they come home with their daily catch.

Doug Porter
Old Counting House Museum,
South Berwick
The Old Berwick Historical Society maintains the Old Counting House Museum next to Salmon Falls River in South Berwick.

LEFT
Janet Mendelsohn
On the Road to Seapoint Beach
Kittery Point
How many generations of Cutts Island boatbuilders have worked in this barn? On the road to Seapoint Beach, its sturdy lines are a magnet for those who, like me, admire the craftsmanship and history it harbors.

Doug Porter
Listed on the National Register of Historic Places, the William Fogg Library on Old Road in Eliot is one of the Town's most prominent buildings.

Doug Porter
Hamilton House Museum,
South Berwick

The grand architecture of Hamilton House in South Berwick beams bright white during a September sunrise. The formal gardens offer a summer concert series on Sunday afternoons. Hamilton House is one of dozens of museum homes operated by the Society for the Preservation of New England Antiquities.

Doug Porter
Salt-water tidal pools fill during Maine's high tides.

Doug Porter
Cornfields glisten a golden color in the bright September sunlight in Eliot.

Doug Porter
A lonesome sailboat is dreaming of being unleashed, to go from its mooring in a tidal pool to catch the winds of the Atlantic Ocean.

RIGHT
Doug Porter
Busy Route 236 in Eliot offers miles of scenic natural beauty if one takes the time to see it.

Doug Porter
The waterfront area of Eliot remains much as it was one hundred years ago.

LEFT
Doug Porter
Grain silos, cornfields and dramatic forests surround you in Eliot.

Doug Porter
*Rolling fields lie serene against
a September sky in this peaceful
setting from Goodwin Road in Eliot.*

RIGHT
Doug Porter
*Step back through time, to a period
when New England shorelines were
ones of natural beauty. That is Eliot
today, preserved and magnificent.*

Doug Porter
Wild purple lavender fills a field in mid-September in Eliot.

Doug Porter
Protected wildlife area. Wildlife abounds in Eliot from its many fresh and salt-water pools and ponds.

Doug Porter

Small family farms dot the rural community of Eliot, Maine. Geese enjoy the afternoon autumn sun.

Mary Ellen McCollumn
First Congregational Church
Kittery Point
Said to be the first church in Maine,
established in 1730.

Doug Porter
Eliot Waterfront

*A glimpse through the trees of
the Piscataqua River in Eliot tends
to relax individuals in this rural community, so close to the hustle and
bustle of the surrounding towns.*

RIGHT

Norma Stevens Carter

*Eliot boat launching on the banks
of the Piscataqua River, Hammond
Lane, Eliot. While attending the
Eliot Chili Festival I could see that
there was going to be a beautiful
sunset. I grabbed my camera and a
friend to enjoy the view and capture
this image.*

THE YORKS

The Town of York lies to the north of Kittery and is comprised of a group of villages, each with its own personality and appeal. "The Yorks" have been home to seafaring folk since the 17th century. Since that time, York Village, York Harbor, York Beach and Cape Neddick have been luring visitors to stay a day, a week, a summer or a lifetime.

See the rugged coastline from York Harbor and view the 1760's Captain Jonathan Sayward house. Beyond the beach the spectacular Cliff Walk awaits, with stately 19th-century homes on one side (many of them now inns and Bed and Breakfasts), and pebble beaches and dramatic coastal views on the other. Walk the two-mile Long Sands Beach at low tide and try the two-mile Brave Boat Harbor Trail.

York Village boasts its ties to earlier times. Clustered within the Village between York Street and the York River, the Old York Historical Society maintains a number of buildings that evoke scenes of earlier local life. The 1710 Old Gaol (Jail) with cells and the gaoler's quarters furnished as in 1790. The Emerson-Wilcox house contains wonderfully furnished period rooms with examples of the best decorative arts of the day. The 1745 Schoolhouse, the John Hancock Warehouse, and the Jefferds Tavern provide the ability to sample educational, commercial and social aspects of 18th century life in York Village. The Elizabeth Perkins House offers a glimpse of life for wealthy summer residents in the late 19th century.

In York Beach, enjoy the enthusiastic Sousa marches of the evening summer concerts at the bandstand. And don't leave without the taste of sweet York Beach saltwater taffy in clean pastel colors.

Visit Sohier Park off Route 1A in Cape Neddick to catch the beautiful views of the Atlantic coast and the cherished and much photographed 1879 Nubble Light (the Cape Neddick Light Station).

Susan Stevens
Mt. Agamenticus, York from the
South Berwick Side
Morning shades of fog.

RIGHT
Mary Ellen McCollumn
York Harbor Beach, York
*The rugged end of a beautiful and
very popular horseshoe-shaped
beach is one of York's splendid
features. Be sure to visit York's two-
mile long stretch of sand and surf at
Long Sands Beach and Short Sands
Beach next to York Harbor Village.*

LEFT
Nancy Page
A Winter Sunset on the York River
Town Wharf, York Harbor
While the area bustles during the tourist season, a winter's day finds it peaceful and seemingly untouched by man. A beautiful location any time of year! Route 103 is the "back road" that winds its way from Kittery to York Harbor, and is a popular route for locals and tourists alike.

Edgar Ohman
Christmas on the Nubble
York
For several years the Cape Neddick Light Station, also known as Nubble Light, has been beautifully illuminated during the Christmas season. On the Saturday after Thanksgiving a late afternoon lighting ceremony is held each year at Sohier Park, with music, caroling and refreshments. During "Yorks Days" at the end of July, the lights are turned on again for one evening of "Christmas in July."

Edgar Ohman
Harbor Beach, York
A short crescent shaped beach off Route 1A in York Harbor. The old "Fisherman's Walk" traverses the rocky and high cliff along the shoreline seen in the background. This is a lovely spot at sunrise and again in the late afternoon.

Mary Ellen McCollumn
Cape Neddick Light Station
Nubble Light, York
*Driving along Route 1A, don't miss
Cape Neddick and the Nubble
Lighthouse at Sohier Park. Said to
be one of Maine's most visited and
photographed lighthouses, it was
originally built in 1879. Standing
137 feet high, it is the tallest lighthouse in Maine. It has been automated
since 1987 and is on the National
Register of Historic Places.*

Leanne Cusimano
Barn off Route 91
York
I lived on the winding country road in York known as Route 91. One autumn day, I decided to detour down a side road that I passed daily, and was rewarded with beautiful views, among them this barn.

Mary Ellen McCollumn
George Marshall's Store
York
Established in 1867, this historic landmark is situated on the York River just off Route 1A. Located near the Hancock Warehouse and Wharf, the building is now an Art Gallery and part of the Museum Buildings of the Old York Historical Society.

Judy Ahearn Salsich
Old Weare Barn on Pine Hill
Old Weare Homestead
Cape Neddick

RIGHT
Judy Ahearn Salsich
*The View from Shirley's Porch:
Barn at Weare Homestead*
Cape Neddick

Edgar Ohman
Cape Neddick Lobster Pound
Cape Neddick
This view of the lobster pound was taken from the small harbor, not navigable at low tide, at the mouth of the Cape Neddick River. Follow Route 1A from York Beach to a fork in the road where the Shore takes the right.

LEFT
Leanne Cusimano
Cape Neddick Lobster Shack
This picture was taken several years ago, when I was relatively new to the area. One of my favorite pastimes was to drive along Shore Road and enjoy the scenery. To me, that marsh and shack feel like "quintessential Maine."

Rose Gotsis
Fishing Shacks
Southern Maine, Route 1A
*I am always attracted to graphic
lines and vivid color. These old
fishing shacks along Route 1A
couldn't be overlooked — they
shouted, "This is Maine."*

Fredrick St. Cyr
The Famous and Majestic Nubble
Light at Cape Neddick
Full sail along the rock-bound coast
of Maine with the wind at your
back and following seas... a true
prescription for beauty and relaxation.

RIGHT TOP
Doug Porter
Long Sands Beach in York Beach
features hundreds of houses avail-
able for weekly rentals.

RIGHT BELOW
Doug Porter
Visiting Short Sands Beach in York
Beach is like stepping back through
time. Salt water Taffy, amusement
parks, grand hotels, sidewalk
cafes and those neat beach shops
are plentiful.

Edgar Ohman
York Congregational Church, York
Built in 1747, this beautiful church is in the heart of York Village across from the Old Burial Ground. York has a wonderful history and is lovely to visit anytime of the year but it is especially peaceful after a winter snowfall.

Lisa Patey
Nubble Light on a Spring Day

RIGHT
Judy Ahearn Salsich
Lazy days of summer at the Old Weare Homestead, Cape Neddick.

Judy Ahearn Salsich
Cape Neddick, York
*The Jeremiah Weare Farmhouse
on Pine Hill Road.*

Mary Ellen McCollumn
Hancock Warehouse
and Wharf, York

Once owned by John Hancock, signer of the Declaration of Independence, it served as the customs house for York. It is now a museum and part of the Museum Buildings of the Old York Historical Society. The Wharf is the winter home for the Captain Edward H. Adams gundalow that is towed to Prescott Park in Portsmouth each summer.

John N. Slipkowsky
Historic Cemetery
York Village

RIGHT
John N. Slipkowsky
Old Jail (Olde Gaol)
York Village

OGUNQUIT

The Algonquin Indians named this place "Negunquit" meaning "Beautiful Place by the Sea." All those who come here year after year to surf, swim, sunbathe, walk, jog and generally have fun are in full agreement. Originally part of Wells, Ogunquit established itself as a summer resort in the 1880's and provided inspiration for artists soon after.

From Ogunquit village center on Route 1 take Beach Street to 3½ miles of white sandy beach and the ocean. Umbrellas, big and small, dot the beach, vividly set against the white sands and sparkling sea. Catch the Fourth of July fireworks lighting the warm summer night sky.

Walk the 1¼ mile Marginal Way along the flower-dotted cliffs, which connects the town with picturesque Perkins Cove, a much-photographed spot. This fishing village has become a haven for artists, though lobster boats still work here and you will find fresh seafood to eat and small shops to tempt your pocketbook. Not to be missed is a visit to the famed Ogunquit Museum of American Art on Shore Road to see its permanent collection, special summer exhibitions, and the sculpture on its pleasant grounds. Take a sightseeing boat trip or a 20-minute walk along Shore Road back to the village. Don't feel like walking? You can always take the trolley — just listen for the bell. North of the village, walk across the famous footbridge and stroll along the beach and sea dunes.

Fine dining is an art in Ogunquit as is a wide range of comfortable accommodations. And follow dinner with a memorable performance at the professional Ogunquit Playhouse, established in 1933 and the summer home to many well-known actors.

Doug Porter
Perkins Cove
Fishing and pleasure boats all point their bows to the open sea.

LEFT
Elizabeth M. Hutz
Perkins Cove, Ogunquit

Susan Stevens
Balancing Rock
A glacial boulder off Emery's Bridge Road, South Berwick near the line of western Ogunquit, 5 miles from Ogunquit Square.

RIGHT
Betty-Jean Collins Cooper
Winter view of Ogunquit footbridge. 1 1/2 miles from the center of Ogunquit at Ocean Street, the footbridge area is very quaint. On our first winter visit to Ogunquit we found it in hibernation, recovering from the past summer, getting ready for the next season.

Bernie O'Doherty
Marginal Way, Ogunquit
January 1, 1997 and 0 degrees producing a brisk, clear and bright day. Just perfect for a long walk along the shore to see the contrast of colors.

RIGHT
John N. Slipkowsky
Beach in Winter
Ogunquit

Doug Porter
Perkins Cove
A perfect September destination.

LEFT
Doug Porter
*The Marginal Way (Cliff Walk)
in Ogunquit allows a brisk bit of
exercise while you view miles of
the Maine coast.*

James Ready
Sunrise through the canopy at Main Beach in Ogunquit at the most beautiful and serene time of day.

LEFT
Judy Ahearn Salsich
Woman with Lobster
(her first in 15 years)
A friend in a pinch. Good eating at the Oarweed Restaurant in Ogunquit

RIGHT
Doug Porter
Low tide along the Marginal Way in Ogunquit. The perfect location to peek into tidal pools and see what Mother Nature has brought. Shows change twice a day.

WELLS

Wells and Moody share seven miles of pristine beach, separated from the commercial bustle of Route 1 by a broad tidal marsh. Such very fine white sands, broad and flat, draw thousands of beach lovers each year to swim, sunbathe, build sandcastles and wade in tidal pools. Watch for the gulls swirling above the solitary sea grasses, noisily demanding to be noticed.

Named for the ancient English cathedral city, Wells began as a Webhannet River mill town, becoming Maine's third incorporated town in 1653. It now comprises 62 square miles with Moody Beach, Wells Beach, Drakes Island, High Pine, Wells Branch and the Merriland Ridge area all part of the greater Wells area.

The Historical Society of Wells owns the historic First Meetinghouse Museum, a National Register landmark, where cultural events take place, artifacts are displayed and the research library is well-used by genealogists. Wells is an antiquarian books and antiques haven. There are boat excursions, free concerts at the Hope Hobbs Gazebo and the Wells Auto Museum to enjoy.

At Wells, too, are the Wells National Estuarine Research Reserve on Laudholm Farm Road and the Rachel Carson National Wildlife Refuge on Route 9. Both are beautiful spots in all seasons with lush vegetation in spring and summer and the crispness of autumn, with its dry leaves bedded down awaiting the approach of winter.

Resorts, inns, ocean-side summer rentals, motels and campgrounds offer a variety of accommodations. There's a wide range and variety of restaurants; and fresh-caught seafood is available everywhere.

Neil Falby
Marking Time
Wells Harbor
Buoys for locating lobster traps.
Buoys of all different shapes and
sizes... and all of them identified by
every imaginable color combination.
They are just as much a symbol and
part of Maine's nautical heritage as
the rocky coastline itself.

RIGHT
Sharon Avdet
Boat Gossips: Wells Harbor
September 1998

Michael Caplan
Dinner Time
Wells Center Beach, Wells
Lunch at a stand in Wells Center, then a walk along the beach. The tide was out and a fresh lunch was also waiting for a few local residents.

LEFT
Michael Caplan
Winter Sculpture
Jetty Beach, Wells
For a seasonal resident of Wells, it is a must to return during the winter to check the old house, take a walk on Wells beach and enjoy the magnificent sand sculptures created by strong winter winds.

RIGHT
Randy Newell
Sunrise at Drakes Island Beach
Wells
It was a brisk spring morning. The sun was coming up, seagulls were patrolling the beach, and the tide was coming in. I was there to watch the waking of the day.

Neil Falby
Shimmering Sunset
Wells Harbor
Like glistening jewels, the sun's last rays of the day reflect in the swirls of the ebbing tide. The colors are in constant motion and seem to dance upon the water. The scene is ever changing…the moment must be captured quickly before darkness prevails.

Neil Falby
First Light
Wells Harbor

*For those who are curious enough...
and make the required 4:30 a.m.
effort...the precious moments just
before sunrise may provide the best
coastal photographic opportunities
of the day. There is no guarantee,
however, that nature will cooperate.
Some of the best conditions include
no wind, a few clouds and a ball of
fire hovering just below the horizon.
Lady Luck provided all three this
morning.*

Neil Falby
Tranquil Reflection
Wells Harbor

Stillness oftentimes stirs the senses. Perceptions sharpen...and we are able to see the true beauty of something that might otherwise be passed by. This mirror-like image, for example, is more than just a reflection. It is a piece of nature's artwork on temporary display. As soon as even the slightest breeze arrives, the show will be over.

RIGHT
Sharon Avdet
Sweet Pea: Sunset in Wells Harbor at the town docks

RIGHT, BELOW
Michael Caplan
Dory in the Fall
Wells Harbor

The mid-October colors of Wells Harbor, the dory, the red sea apple blossoms, the calm blue-green water and the yellow sea grass make a wonderful fall experience.

Doug Porter
Moody Beach leading to Ogunquit Beach offers large rambling beach houses clustered at the Maine shore. Wild roses bloom from May to October.

LEFT
Janet Mendelsohn
Rachel Carson National Wildlife Refuge, Wells
It would be easy to romanticize this place where Chauncey Creek sweeps in and out of Rachel Carson Wildlife Refuge. But in truth, it is serene, peaceful, at all times of the day, in all seasons.

Randy Newell
*Private Flower Garden
on Drakes Island*
*Sitting by the pool, looking at
the flowers and watching the bees,
I noticed this bee just enjoying the
sun. It seemed to capture the
essence of the lazy day.*

RIGHT
Sharon Avdet
*Queen Anne's Lace:
Old Barn on Route 1*
Wells in July.

James Ready
A doe feeding in Laudholm Farm Nature Preserve, Wells. If it weren't for Laudholm Farm, scenes like this of the white-tailed deer would not take place. Food, shelter, thick woods and open fields protect their way of life.

LEFT
Sharon Avdet
Satisfaction
Seal in Wells Harbor seen from a boat while fishing

Janice Powell
Laudholm Farm Preserve, Wells
Woodland on one of the last surviving
saltwater farms in Southern Maine.

RIGHT
James Ready
Shades of Wyeth?
Laudholm Farm Preserve, Wells
This wooden trail goes from a wide,
open meadow, through a thick
forest and a salt marsh to a beach.
A must see.

Janice Powell
Rachel Carson Preserve, Wells
*Tidal marshes and rivers lead to
the ocean. The foreground offers
a window-like view.*

LEFT
Sharon Avdet
March: Wells Harbor

RIGHT
Sharon Avdet
After the Storm
*In a small park on Route 1, normally
a tiny waterfall, this swelled after a
heavy October rain.*

LEFT
Susan Stevens
Wells Division 6 Schoolhouse
Tatnic Road, Wells
2 miles west of Route 1.

ABOVE
Neil Falby
Frozen Summer Memories
Wells Beach
*Maine's near zero temperature has
transformed summer's playful surf
spray into an intricate honeycomb
of ice. Absent are the gleeful shrills
of children splashing in the waves.
Gone, too, are the ritualistic
"beach walkers." No one is sunning
on the deck today either! But if
winter comes can spring...or
summer...be far behind?*

LEFT
Randy Newell
Salt Marsh on Drakes Island Rd
*It was a cold winter day all; seemed
deserted; everything was still. As the
sun set, it got colder and quiet. The
marsh was preparing to sleep for
the night.*

ABOVE
Edward W. Greene, Jr
Ice Storm 1998
Chapel Road, Wells

THE KENNEBUNKS

The oceanfront communities of Kennebunk and Kennebunkport have been popular summer resorts for many decades.

More than two dozen sites are within Kennebunk's National Historic Register District. Trees shade streets of 18th and 19th century houses built by merchants and sea captains. Elegant and comfortable accommodations are to be found here, as many homes have become inns and Bed and Breakfasts. The town has been popular with writers and artists for many years: both Kenneth Roberts (born in nearby Kennebunk) and Booth Tarkington wrote about Kennebunkport.

The Kennebunk Historical Society offers guided architectural walking tours of this popular oceanfront community, and there's so much else to see. The Walkers Point estate of former President and Mrs. George Bush attracts strollers on Parsons Way.

Getting around town is easy on foot, by car, bike or trolley, and fine restaurants and casual eating places abound. Ocean Avenue from Dock Square, whose restored buildings house many boutiques, galleries and shops, affords drivers a picturesque tour of the coastline. The long, wide sands of Kennebunk, Mother's and Gooch's Beaches delight those who like to walk, play in the surf and sun themselves. There is a wide choice of deep-sea fishing and whale-watching trips and guided ocean and river kayaking adventures.

The Seashore Trolley Museum on the Log Cabin Road traces the history of the electric trolley and other public transit vehicles. The Kennebunk Maritime Museum and Gallery is a popular attraction as is the Franciscan Monastery that offers serenity in its chapel, shrines and gardens.

The full calendar of cultural and fun events requires that vacationers return year after year. Return in late fall to enjoy the tranquillity and beauty of this community and in the winter to celebrate holiday seasons of yesteryear at the annual Christmas Prelude.

Janice Powell
Cape Porpoise Harbor,
Kennebunkport *A working fisherman's harbor with several small
islands dotting the entrance. Taken
in late afternoon in the Spring. The
harbor waters were calm, glassy,
clear blue and reflective; an ethereal
quality of the day.*

LEFT
Janice Powell
Cape Porpoise Harbor,
Kennebunkport

RIGHT
Robert Dennis
Morning Reflection
Cape Porpoise
*Waking up on a clear and beautiful
summer morning, who could resist a
waiting sailboat, still water, pleasant
scenery, and their invitation to a
leisurely cruise to sea?*

Janice Powell
Beach Rose
Parsons Beach, Kennebunkport
This rose bush is seen along many beaches, dunes and marshes. Flowers develop profusely in the early summer and by mid-summer the berries or "rose-hips" are growing. The berries are just as beautiful as the flowers.

Janice Powell
Beach Rose
Goose Rocks Beach, Kennebunkport
It is rare to find such fine white sand as seen here. In June the first blooms of roses come out, fresh green and flowering, draping over the beautiful sand.

RIGHT TOP
Janice Powell
Asters
Parson's Beach, Kennebunkport
Seen in delicate bunches along paths, beaches, and roadways during September and October.

RIGHT BELOW
Janice Powell
Kennebunkport
Lady Slipper after a rainstorm.

Neil Falby
Lobster Country
Cape Porpoise
Occasionally, the Southern Maine coast serves up a perfect summer day. A deep blue sky is speckled with a few puffy clouds to add interest. Colors everywhere are clear and vivid. Visibility is unlimited. What a memorable combination! On this day, the spectacular weather will help make pulling and setting the lobster traps a little easier.

LEFT
Bernie O'Doherty
Cape Porpoise, Kennebunk
Mid-morning reflections. It looked like a dream; I played along and captured it.

RIGHT
Mary F Woodman
The Red Boat
Kennebunkport
Kennebunk River with River Club in the background.

Robert Dennis
Lupine along Ocean Ave,
Kennebunkport
*The early-June blooming of lupine
along the Maine coast brings a
welcome splash of color and is a
harbinger of summer.*

RIGHT
Robert Dennis
Boats at Rest
Kennebunk River
*Cape Porpoise: the stillness of the
early morning hours is often the
best time to capture the area's
unique charms.*

Barbara Risdon Adams
Grounds of the Shawmut Inn
Resort
This open seaside field of yellow
coreopsis seemed to shout
at me - "This is Nature's Pot of Gold
at the end of the rainbow, please
snap us so that others may also
enjoy." I found the view to be
spiritually uplifting.

RIGHT TOP
Elizabeth M. Hutz
Flower Farm, Route 1,
South Kennebunk

RIGHT BELOW
Robert Dennis
4th of July in Historic
Kennebunkport
Kennebunkport is blessed with
many distinctive and historic homes
from the late 18th and early 19th
centuries. Many of them, like this
one built in 1795, carry a special
message on the Fourth of July.

Robert Dennis
Winter Surf
Ocean Avenue, Kennebunkport
The majestic surf after a winter storm is an awesome sight to behold - and can also be a dangerous one for onlookers.

Robert Dennis
Sea Roses
Ocean Ave, Kennebunkport
Sea roses blooming in mid-June herald the arrival of another beautiful summer.

LEFT
Mark W. Ettinger
Apple Collecting
Gile Orchard, Alfred
It was one of those perfect fall days. The kind you want to spend in an orchard. It was time for our annual father-son apple-picking trip. The hard part was trying to keep it to one bushel of "prize" apples.

TOP LEFT
Janice Powell
Dories at Sunset
Kennebunkport
The dories are a reminder of the fishing tradition in Maine and this area. The setting sun was reflecting on everything In the scene giving it a shining glow.

Bernie O'Doherty
Barnard's Tavern 1776,
Kennebunk
A walk back in time, capturing a slice of living, breathing history. The architecture bespeaks the time period. Stopped traffic to get this one!

RIGHT
James Ready
Autumn Sonata:
At the Franciscan Monastery
Kennebunk
Exquisite and peaceful in all seasons.

Bernie O'Doherty
Goose Rocks Beach at Dawn
Woke up early one summer morning; saw that the sky was looking promising and raced down to the beach. Ran across the sands and captured it. Thirty seconds later the magic was gone.

BELOW
Bernie O'Doherty
Batson River, Cape Porpoise
A quiet sunset by the river. It is more like a large stream, with minimum water flow. Very peaceful and quiet, except for the mosquitoes!!

LEFT
Neil Falby
Foggy Wash Day
Cape Porpoise
Lobstermen are like the legendary mail carriers—neither rain nor wind nor sleet...nor fog...deters them from their tasks. Today the fog brings with it a different mood and an interesting change of activities within the harbor. Few, if any, boats have left their mooring. It's the perfect time to scrape the barnacles and debris off the buoys...followed by a wash and a rinse. Although it's too risky to journey to the sea, hands are never idle and time is never wasted...no matter what the weather.

Mark W. Ettinger
Nature through a Child's Eye
Perfect foliage, Perfect light, Perfect Kodak moment. My son Jesse was pretending to fish on the banks of the Mousam River in West Kennebunk. I clicked the shutter and knew I had captured something very special. It was an almost surreal setting.

LEFT
Carol Hartley Bellows
Frankie
Fawncrest Meadows near Kennebunk, Maine
Frankie has become a favored friend at Fawncrest Meadows near Kennebunk.

Carol Hartley Bellows
Fall - A Performance of Peace
Stroll Alone, Look Up and No
Longer Feel Alone. The Sky, The
Trees, The Fields of Life Await A
Handshake and A Smile - Fawncrest
Meadows near Kennebunk, Maine.

RIGHT
Bernie O'Doherty
Wallingford Farm, Kennebunk
*For me it expressed the Zen of Fall –
colors, hues, history and time
passed. Put on the brakes, pulled
over and shot it!*

LEFT
Robert Dennis
Fall in Cape Porpoise
The colors of the season and the area's unique seacoast charm make for scenes of special beauty.

ABOVE
Robert Dennis
Autumn Reflections - Cape Porpoise
In the fall, the Maine coast offers scenes of classic beauty second to none in New England.

RIGHT
Robert Dennis
Bush-watchers
Walker Point, Kennebunkport
Tourists often focus on Walker Point, summer home of former President Bush, to the exclusion of many other scenic parts of town, but, then again, it is a very dramatic site in its own right.

Elizabeth M. Hutz
Roger's Pond, Kennebunk

RIGHT
Robert Dennis
Fall in Cape Porpoise
*Early morning hours provide the
best time to capture the stillness of
the Kennebunk River and the colors
of fall.*

Robert Dennis
Boats at Rest
Cape Porpoise
Winter in Cape Porpoise: The Maine coast offers lasting images of beauty in all seasons.

LEFT
Robert Dennis
Carolers, Christmas Prelude
Dock Square, Kennebunkport
Every year, Kennebunkport's Christmas Prelude draws thousands from near and far to this classic New England village to join in traditional holiday celebrations.

RIGHT
Robert Dennis
Winter Surf
Ocean Avenue, Kennebunkport
Winter along the Maine coast can also offer scenes of quiet beauty.

LEFT
Bernie O'Doherty
Batson River, Cape Porpoise
*It was so quiet, the camera click
sounded like an explosion.*

BELOW
Judy Ahearn Salsich
Kennebunk Cemetery
*View from behind the Kennebunk
library - intimations of our immortality?*

RIGHT
Bernie O'Doherty
Goose Rocks Beach, Kennebunk
*Just after sunset. I came around the
bend from Timber Point and was
struck at the sight. I had to snap out
of it so I could snap it. A minute
later the magic was gone.*

INDEX OF PHOTOGRAPHERS